Pebble

Dogs

Beagles

by Jody Sullivan Rake

Consulting Editor: Gail Saunders-Smith, PhD

Consultant: Jennifer Zablotny, DVM
Member, American Veterinary Medical Association

Capstone
press
Mankato, Minnesota

Pebble Books are published by Capstone Press,
151 Good Counsel Drive, P.O. Box 669, Mankato, Minnesota 56002.
www.capstonepress.com

1 2 3 4 5 6 11 10 09 08 07 06

Library of Congress Cataloging-in-Publication Data
Rake, Jody Sullivan.
   Beagles / by Jody Sullivan Rake.
   p. cm.—(Pebble Books. Dogs)
   Summary: "Simple text and photographs present an introduction to the beagle
breed, its growth from puppy to adult, and pet care information"—Provided by
publisher.
   Includes bibliographical references and index.
   ISBN-13: 978-0-7368-5330-9 (hardcover)
   ISBN-10: 0-7368-5330-8 (hardcover)
   1. Beagle (Dog breed) I. Title. II. Series.
SF429.B3R35 2006
636.753'7—dc22   2005023968

Note to Parents and Teachers

The Dogs set supports national science standards related to life
science. This book describes and illustrates beagles. The images
support early readers in understanding the text. The repetition of
words and phrases helps early readers learn new words. This book
also introduces early readers to subject-specific vocabulary words,
which are defined in the Glossary section. Early readers may need
assistance to read some words and to use the Table of Contents,
Glossary, Read More, Internet Sites, and Index sections of the book.

Table of Contents

Super Sniffers

Beagles like to sniff.
They have a good
sense of smell.

Some beagles work
at airports.
They sniff bags
for unsafe items.

From Puppy to Adult

Beagle puppies are
very curious.
They learn
about the world
by sniffing everything.

Beagle puppies drink milk from their mothers. They grow quickly.

Adult beagles
are small dogs.
They are a little taller
than one stair.

Taking Care of Beagles

Beagles have short fur. Owners should brush their beagles often.

Beagles are full of energy.
Owners should walk
their beagles every day.

Beagles are thirsty
after exercise.
They need water and
food every day.

Beagles love
sniffing and playing.
Beagles are great pets.

Glossary

curious—wanting to learn and investigate, interested in new things

energy—the ability to work and play for a long time, not getting tired easily

sense—a way of knowing about one's surroundings; seeing, hearing, touching, tasting, and smelling are the five senses.

sniff—to breathe in through the nose for smelling

Read More

Murray, Julie. *Beagles.* Animal Kingdom. Edina, Minn.: Abdo, 2002.

Trumbauer, Lisa. *The Life Cycle of a Dog.* Life Cycles. Mankato, Minn.: Pebble Books, 2002.

Internet Sites

FactHound offers a safe, fun way to find Internet sites related to this book. All of the sites on FactHound have been researched by our staff.

Here's how:

1. Visit *www.facthound.com*

2. Type in this special code **0736853308** for age-appropriate sites. Or enter a search word related to this book for a more general search.

3. Click on the **Fetch It** button.

FactHound will fetch the best sites for you!

Index

Word Count: 101

Grade: 1

Early-Intervention Level: 14

Editorial Credits

Martha E. H. Rustad, editor; Juliette Peters, designer; Jo Miller, photo researcher;
Scott Thoms, photo editor

Photo Credits